巴拉克·奧巴馬

Heroes and Role Models | Non-Fiction Series

Copyright © 2022 by Level Learning, INC. and Washington Yu Ying PCS™
Original and Edited Text Copyright © 2022 by Washington Yu Ying PCS™

All rights reserved. No part of this book in whole or part may be reproduced without written permission from the publisher.

Published by Level Learning, INC.
Content Contributors:
Washington Yu Ying PCS™ - Teng Shen, Pearl Zao He You
Level Learning - Jingyao Qi

Illustrations by: Matt Austin

Leveling classification based on Level Learning standard.
For full description, visit www.levellearning.com

ISBN 978-1-64040-047-4
Traditional Chinese Edition

About Level Learning:
Level Learning provides a literacy focused curriculum specifically designed for K-12 Chinese as a Second Language classrooms. Our program offers 20 levels of specific and detailed objectives, leveled texts and passages, mastery-based online assessment, and analytics to enable data-driven instruction. Level Learning reading curriculum for both literature and informational text emphasize grammar and comprehension skills to help teachers develop confident and independent Chinese language readers. The non-fiction series of books are specifically designed to support our informational text course based on multiple national standards. To learn more about our entire offering, visit www.levellearning.com.

About Washington Yu Ying PCS™:
Washington Yu Ying PCS is a Mandarin English dual language immersion International Baccalaureate (IB) World school. Yu Ying's mission is to inspire and prepare young people to create a better world by challenging them to reach their full potential in a nurturing Chinese/English educational environment. Yu Ying's comprehensive IB, dual immersion curriculum equips students with global competencies for success in the real world. As a leader in immersion education, Yu Ying is determined to advance Chinese language programs and global citizenry education by helping other schools create and strengthen their Chinese programs. For more information, email: products@washingtonyuying.org

巴拉克·奧巴馬是美國第44任總統。他也是美國第一任非洲裔總統。

1961年,奧巴馬出生在美國的夏威夷州。小時候的奧巴馬因為自己的膚色,經常受到不公平的對待,這讓他很難過。

奥巴馬從紐約市哥倫比亞大學畢業以後，來到芝加哥工作。那時候，他幫助了很多當地的窮人。為了幫助更多的人，他想要成為一名律師。所以，他又去了哈佛大學法律系學習。

奥巴马從哈佛大學畢業後，又回到了芝加哥工作。1996年，奥巴馬被選為伊利諾伊州參議員，2004年，他成為美國參議院的參議員。

2008年,奧巴馬成為美國總統。在他的努力下,美國和伊拉克的戰爭結束了。2009年,他得到了「諾貝爾和平獎」。

奥巴马關心人民的平等權利，在他當總統時，他提高最低收入，減少稅收，他還提出了新的醫療法案。他的很多做法都受到美國人民的歡迎。

2017年1月,奧巴馬八年的總統工作結束了。在他的告別演講裡,他鼓勵人們繼續為自由和平等而努力。

Glossary

	Pinyin	English Definition
總統	zǒng tǒng	president
非洲裔	fēi zhōu yì	African descent
夏威夷州	xià wēi yí zhōu	State of Hawaii
膚色	fū sè	skin color
公平	gōng píng	equally
對待	duì dài	treatment
難過	nán guò	sad
紐約市	niǔ yuē shì	New York City
哥倫比亞大學	gē lún bǐ yà dà xué	Columbia University
畢業	bì yè	to graduate
芝加哥	zhī jiā gē	Chicago
律師	lǜ shī	lawyer
哈佛大學	hā fó dà xué	Harvard University
法律系	fǎ lǜ xì	law school

	Pinyin	English Definition
伊利諾伊州	yī lì nuò yī zhōu	Illinois
參議員	cān yì yuán	senator
美國參議院	měi guó cān yì yuàn	Unites States Senate
伊拉克	yī lā kè	Iraq
戰爭	zhàn zhēng	war
結束	jié shù	end
諾貝爾和平獎	nuò bèi ěr hé píng jiǎng	Nobel Peace Prize
平等權利	píng děng quán lì	equal rights
最低收入	zuì dī shōu rù	minimum wage
稅收	shuì shōu	tax
提出	tí chū	to propose
醫療	yī liáo	medical care
法案	fǎ àn	law

	Pinyin	English Definition
受到	shòu dào	to receive
告別	gào bié	farewell
演講	yǎn jiǎng	speech
鼓勵	gù lì	to encourage
自由	zì yóu	freedom

www.ingramcontent.com/pod-product-compliance
Lightning Source LLC
Chambersburg PA
CBHW041224070526
44584CB00001B/89